Published by Rock N' Roll Colouring Ltd® 2021

© 2021 Thin Lizzy under license by Thin Lizzy Ltd.

Designer: Mark Leary at Asylumseventy7
featuring the art of Jim Fitzpatrick with his kind co-operation.

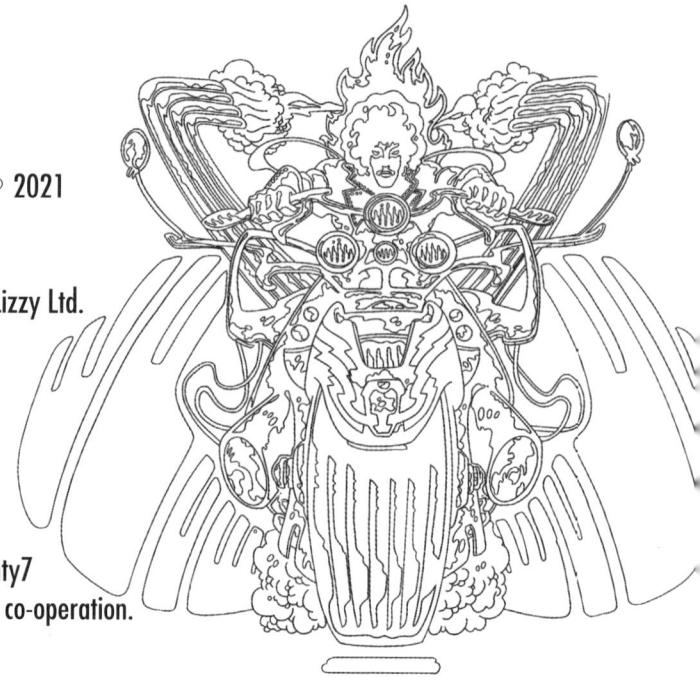

First published in the UK by Rock N' Roll Colouring Ltd®
London
www.rocknrollcolouring.com

ISBN: 9781838147020

Printed in the UK by W&G Baird

The Official Thin Lizzy Colouring Book

TIN LIZZY

ROCK N' ROLL COLOURING

THIN LIZZY

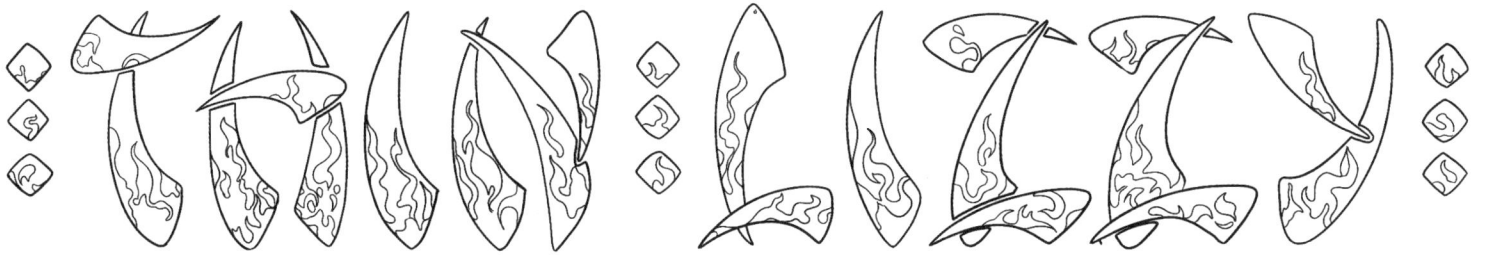

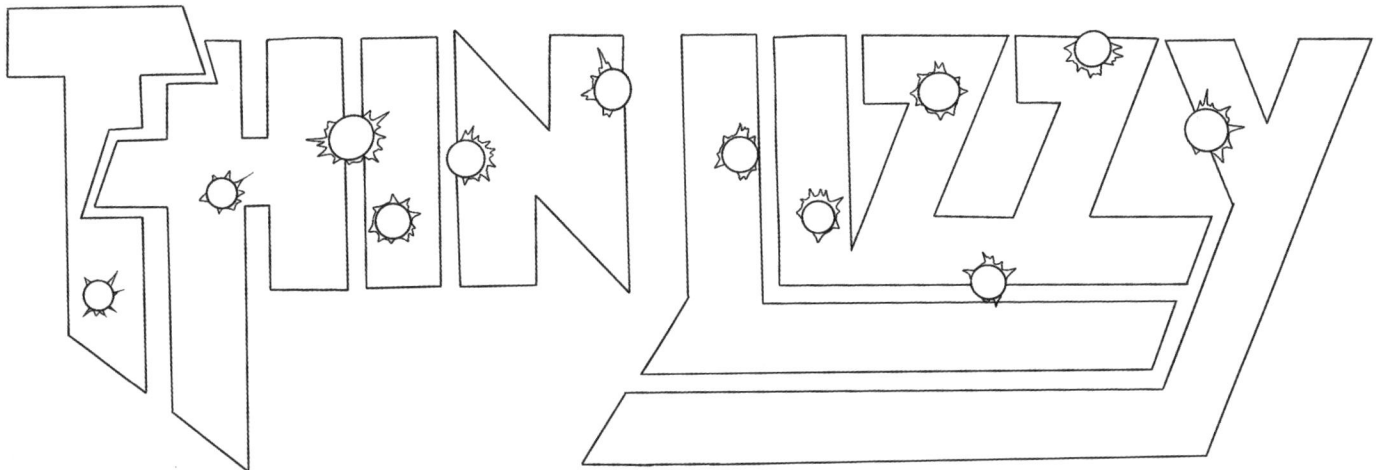

Róisín Dubh

THIN LIZZY
JOHNNY THE FOX

THIN
LIZZY

THIN
LIZZY

For your doodles